About the Author

Gina Rose, an American author currently based in Atlanta, finds inspiration in art, literature, and her yoga practice. Beyond creative and spiritual pursuits, she is driven by a profound commitment to making the world a better place. *"Captivated by life's exquisite beauty juxtaposed with its despair and chaos, poetry is the vessel through which I capture and convey these ineffable truths." -Gina Rose*

Respect the Thorn
Poetry
by Gina Rose

Respect the Thorn Poetry

Gina Rose

Vanguard Press

A CIP catalogue record for this title is
available from the British Library.

ISBN 978 1 80016 952 4

Vanguard Press is an imprint of
Pegasus Elliot Mackenzie Publishers Ltd.
www.pegasuspublishers.com

First Published in 2024

Vanguard Press
Sheraton House Castle Park
Cambridge England

Printed & Bound in Great Britain

Dedication

To the family of my youth who watered my soil and grew my stem, even the ones who tried to drown me. To those who have been poked by my thorn and love me anyway, you know who you are. To my daughter who gave me a reason to seek the petal, even when I didn't want to.

Acknowledgements

To my daughter, Lilli, you are the oxygen in my air. To my mother, Cecelia, your unwavering support when I least expected it carried me like a raft when I was lost at sea.

Contents

Take 1	17
The Stem	19
Childhood Trails	20
Dear Life	22
Migration	25
My Mother was a Dream	30
Invisible Child	33
Journey on Cactus	35
Take 2	39
The Thorn	41
Can't Sing	42
My Friend Who Sits on the Edge	45
Be Wary of the Sharks My Love	47
My Scars Hate the Rain	51
Sounds of the Night Beat in the Day	52
Must Fly	54
Poem from a Tooth	56
Old Miser Time	59
Living in the Gray	61

Crosshairs 62

Pack Animals 65

Devil's Advocate 67

Don't Marry Men Whose Mothers Don't Love Them
69

Burning of Coal 70

Blocked Your Phone 72

Alone 75

I Gave up a lot of Freedom to be Free 76

Take 3 79

The Petal 81

Religion 82

Brooms of Cinnamon 85

Candy Apple Cheeks 87

Someplace Beautiful 90

Mystic Rhyme 92

Squeezing of Clay 94

Colours of Pigment 96

New Moon 97

Let Go 99

Canoe 101

Nobody Complains of Pooping 103

The Road Less Travelled 106

A Christmas Wish 107

Sleep Ever So Sweet	109
Sweep Me Off My Feet	111
Letter to my Lover	113
Sleep in the Nude	116
Tread Softly Sweet Tommy	118
Excerpts	120
Song For My Child	121
Don't Lie	124
Stuck in a Moment	125
Writing You Love Letters	127
Free Verse	129
Life's Answers	131
Not Bored	132
Infinite Darkness	133
Can you Feel It?	134
Life Shouts	135
End	136

Dear Poetry,
My cathartic pastime; I come home to you for healing
and guidance. I know you'll see me through.

Dear Life,
Chew me up and spit me out just please don't take my
wings.

Dear Me,
Shut up and write.

Take 1

The Stem

Journey back to the root, the starting, the seed
    Black-haired child born, struggling to read
Exposing, causes of the growth
    Breaking gypsy oath
Rug moved away, look all that's swept under
    Confusion of life left the child to wonder
            What causes such madness?
    Foundation of youth smothered with sadness
Follow the stem-like yellow brick road
To story of past, story untold.

Childhood Trails

Where the ceilings are bumpy and the fences are chain
    Air is dry in this brown terrain
Vegetables are buttered, all covered and stewed
    Coffee from red can, freshly brewed
Cookies for breakfast, vanilla breeze in the air
    People comfortable with odd stripes in their hair
Flights of high prices, one stop or more
People coming and going without knocks at the door
    Stress for no reason Complaints of each season
    Weird metal hangers, wind in your hair
    Bars that don't close, homeless that stare
    Dusty dirt paths leave prickles in your socks
No lines and landscaping that's covered with rocks

The biggest little city of sin and small dreams
    Be careful where you find comfort,
        things aren't what they seem
TV always running, smoke in the air
    Clean doesn't sparkle and no one seems to care
Where the soap's Irish spring green
    I find evidence at every scene
        Of a life left behind

Not good nor bad, for those things are always with
me, maps in my mind
But of childish naïveté
A scared injured girl able to find joy in play

Just one more story
A small life bred in dust looking for glory
Leaving doubt in my mind these childhood trails
Joys of then hard to feel now but the wounds still
there healing like snails
The need ever present yet ready to flee
Why must we walk these childhood trails—For healing?
For answers? For closure, can it be?
Or just to leave more questions to keep
trying to answer?
Ever evolving as cancer
Some doors shut; others now open
Some closure one day?
Here's to hopin'.

Dear Life

Chew me up and spit me out just please don't take my wings
  If they're wet I know they'll dry, some hope that notion brings
When the wind howls I can spread them and glide
  When the predators stalk I can wrap myself and hide
Times my mind won't rest
  Times my emotions put me to the test
    My wings distract me from my jitters
  When the dust fills the air my wings take me to a place that glitters
The fabric may be torn
  The heat can scorch and burn
    But at least I know they're there
      For if that's so I know I can repair
        But if they're gone I can't go on
          My hope will be lost, all my faith gone
Once I thought I lost them, life gave me a little glimpse My heart so lost being carried away by demons steering blimps
  They knew without my wings to shield me, I was all as good as dead
    They came to finish the job, playing their tricks in my head
The horror that I saw and felt was terrifying at best

The sight of demons, a hellish death tearing at my
chest
My organs twisted, mind collapsed, I couldn't bear
the pain
My scream, my shout could not be heard; no point was
there to strain

Then by some chance, a miracle perhaps
An angel took me under her flaps
She decided to remind me and gave those demons
a swat
*Your wings aren't gone, they just got
caught*
Tangled in this net
*Steer clear of these from now on it's not worth the
bet*

How great it felt to have them back
I twisted I fluttered brushing off the plaque
It took me a while to regain their strength
Stretching regularly and practising daily till they
regained some length
But it taught me so much, that fretful night when I thought
they went away
Without them I can't go on, a block of my airway
To keep them close and cherish them so
Practise every day what I need to never let them go
To find joy in the mundane, what a gift
Never get lost enough for the demons to find you adrift

So knock me down and take my things
But please life, don't take my wings.

Migration

In Chicago it seemed corruption ran deep
Pavers, mobster, gypsies, politicians it'd seep

Snow stood taller than me when we left
Mom had dreams of going West instead

A pewter '87 Lincoln lead our migration
Big Red cinnamon gum pick-ups at every station

This 24-hour town was supposed to be our escape
   From the man singing Hall and Oats on cassette tape
     But he was the one driving us there
       The man with the belt and no hair

A one-bedroom duplex near train tracks would be our den
Our driver heading back to work with other paving men

Three cubs in the room and mother on couch
Short periods of freedom from the belty old grouch

With grandma next door and new cousins to play
It seemed a good thing, this new place that we lay
But the town never slept, it was available twenty-four
   seven
Belt man would be let back in, so certainly this was no
   heaven

When break-ins, poor education, and space became wary
     We moved northwest of town to space that felt airy
          Not knowing the outcome would be nothing short
of hairy

Belt man came and went; that was scary

          A wave of his weapon and threat that would vary

     Finally she'd leave him, 20 years was enough
     I'm sure it was hard but by then she'd grown tough
          Plus she had him, the grizzly to warm her
          She'd discover his drinks that made words slur
               Perhaps it did more, maybe memories it
          blurred
               Though it seemed darkness it stirred
Those first few years were happy
Before wine turned comments to snappy
     And before us children became to scrappy

Trips and new things we never could dream up
Steaks and cherry cokes filling red plastic cups

     Life had a plan, regardless of reason
     Memories turned to pain and the passing of season
Fall-outs, misunderstandings, everyone thinking they are
     right
Yes please I'll take that one-way flight

To something different, over the rainbow
No bluebirds but snow
I didn't care, it was so much different then I'd known

But back to the story
The grizzly man and a few good years of glory
The eldest would stir
Life would be too much for her
She wouldn't go quietly; she'd hurt on the way
The clouds that she'd leave were dark and grey
Us teens stopped playing
No one cared what we were saying
The hurt and confusion of life in this place
Back then if you mentioned it you'd be a disgrace

Talking about your feelings we didn't do back then
It also mattered little the harassment of men
Well what did you do that gave him that notion?
Apparently young girls had a magic potion
Possessing those around to do heinous things
Perhaps from years of history being run by kings
Confusion from all the injustice of life
Created tension, hardness, internal strife
Most of us would stay, some would leave
Innocents of a merry Christmas Eve we'd all grieve

Most of us did well considering the cards we were
dealt
Some stopped eating to deal with the feelings that they
felt
Others seemed not bothered from this castaway place
Some so affected they left not a trace

I never looked back, not till I had to
Until life flipped me the bird and sent me back to that
zoo
     Fifteen years later sitting here with new eyes
       To have this knowledge then would have been
    wise
But I didn't and couldn't have known the good that was
hidden
    It was all I could do to keep my head from spinnin'
This place I now visit still gives me such strain
    The gnawing of memories nipping my brain
      So many good, yet too many bad
        People I left now dying, feelings of sad
It's so close to hell some would say you see Sparks
    To those that stayed they hate these remarks
    The pride that they feel in this Wild West town
      They could care less that everything around is
brown
Alcohol runs at all hours of night
    No stars to be seen in the sky from fake light
This first migration to this dwelling
    Was a foreshadowing that was telling

I would look for my place in this world till I found it
This was my first stop and it gave me my grit
A knowing that what life throws I could handle it.

My Mother was a Dream

My mother was like a dream
　　Always coming and going as it seems
　　　　She would swoop me up and make me sing
　　　　Letting me know the happiness life could bring
We would play and shop
　　Fall and tumble, pretending my hair was a mop
　　　　She loved flowers and the sun
　　Then just as quickly as it had begun
　　　　She'd smile and disappear
　　　　　　I would call and call but my voice she
　　could not hear
I was alone and afraid
　　Remembering when she was near putting my hair in a
　　braid
I would feel her touch and smell her smell
　　As I closed my eyes to remember her spell
　　　　I felt so small and unsure
　　　　　　As I longed to be wrapped in her allure

I would carry on; each day the longing changed
　　Then just like that, my heart would be rearranged
　　　　As she would appear out of the blue
　　　　　　And just like a dream her behaviour I had
　　　　no clue
　　　　　　A dark cloud with threatening Skies?
　　Or an angel embracing me with comforting eyes?

How long would she stay? Would I know this version?
If I was good could I change the
recursion?
Could I get her to stay?
And again get her to laugh and play?
But like a dream I knew I could not control
The knight and shining armour or the troll
Here contented or here blue?
As badly as I tried to
The behaviour could never be predicted
The struggle of all those who love the
addicted
Promises and goals
Or clawing out to go back down the hole
I wonder if she ever even knew
Maybe she just did and never thought
Maybe that's the clue
For does the baby think for the bottle to be brought
I must cry or does he simply let out a coo
No premeditated thought, just an urge that must let out
The when or the why does not matter
Yet it's taught so many, making them sadder
Do we think if we understand the why it would make sense
If there was an apology and change could we truly
recompense?
The puppet master pulling on those memory strings make
them pop up unannounced
It won't go away, no apology, no amends, no drug
renounced

Pain may fade or perhaps just changed

Damage long term, just another relationship estranged.

Invisible Child

No one cares what I have to say
They notice not if my heart aches or longs to play
        Everyone's just concerned with themselves
        Everyone thinking they are Santa when in fact they're
        all elves
Talking over each other, no one is listening;
        The snow on the mountains sitting glistening
Unaffected by these issues, why can't I be more like that?
Not caring of depth just concerned with idle chat

Why should it bother me, no one has to understand
But we were supposed to be close, like members in a band
        They weren't supposed to cut me off mid-feeling
These situations hurt so bad with no sign of healing
My ideas have too many layers
        And their strange games have too many players
        Far too many in their corner
        In this land I'm the foreigner
        I could pretend to fit
                But the thought makes my heart split
        So different, so bizarre
Loneliness is never very far
        No connection here, only conflict
        Outcome I can always predict
        Every time I try to connect I fail
                Nobody hears me when I wail

Invisible I am although in plain sight I will not surround
myself any longer by people who can't see
I will take flight;
I will flee.

Journey on Cactus

When I was a child I remember it blooming
   The first love I had from birth ensuing
   The greatest of all is your first love they utter
   Feeling in chest and stomach that fluttered
Every time that she spoke a singing of song
   Even when scolded for doings of wrong
   The love I felt so strong
   I could burst
   Approval my longing my thirst
I would come to her bed feeling safe in her warmth
   But she would stop letting me in I'd have to go forth;

My second I reckon was the eldest of us
   Excitement, emotion, she made beautiful fuss
   Her enchantment mesmerising
   Emotions uncompromising
This love I learned early was precarious
   Not for the faint of heart Aquarius
   This love was strong
Then poof it was gone
Comfort not to be found at night nor dawn;

Third in my discovery of loves instrument
A steady pillar not driven by stimulant
   A blonde little boy

Basketball his toy
He would be there to relieve not add to the struggle
            Not one to hug, not long would he snuggle
I would sleep top bunk or next to his bed
        But quickly was alone while resting my head—

Sleep much I did never, night tortures only bloomed
            So my forth love came, or so I assumed
It's hard to tell because this looked and felt so new
            Love it was, as far as my view

This road I never drove
        Still head first in I dove
            So happy I did, I finally I had found it
                    To hold me at night the perfect fit
            But almost as quickly as it had begun
            His comforting sting quickly stung
His arms let me go as his back turned to me
        By now she was brewing, the little pea;

My fifth love, the purest, the sweetest so dear
One that brings me most comfort and the most fear
Seven pounds and six ounces and twenty-one inches long
        A love I never felt, an entirely different song
                The peace at night finally here
            She likes to be close, she likes to stay near
She would snuggle on my chest and squeeze me at night
        Little arms so soft, porcelain skin so white
My heart finally full, overflowing with joy

But she is a child, she is not my toy

I feel her growing already away from me each day
        Only a matter of time now my hair's turning grey
        Soon she won't want my comfort under the moon
It's happening fast it's coming soon
Already I find myself alone staring at the ceiling
        Let her blossom, these feelings I'm dealing
She will fly shortly leaving my nest
        Time with her is worth this pain, the joyous the best…

So lie here I do awake under stars
        A million miles away, might as well be on Mars
        A satellite floating amongst a trillion at sea
No one else aboard, no companion for me
Keep looking I decide for something new not a person
        Notion of this makes the pain worsen
            Perhaps a new love I never knew exists
        One that won't leave me, one that persists
Books perhaps, a god, a practice?
        The pursuit of happiness, journey on cactus.

Take 2

The Thorn

Enjoyable it's not, it stings the flesh
Grown to keep things out
    Created to bring about doubt
        This barrier was born
            Here it is, here's the thorn
        Sting my flesh
     Lemon drops on a cut
Reminder to keep guarded
    Not to open up
Ugly and rough
    A wolf costume to scare
        Warning to all heed and beware
The cut is real, it is precise and ready
    If you can get through that, the rest isn't so heavy
The thorn is here approach it you dare
The smell as pleasant as burning of hair.

Can't Sing

The me that once was is being ripped out,
    thrown from my chest
My will to carry on being questioned,
    every second a test
The me that once was is painfully dying
    Soul strains to hang on
      the fight has me laying here crying

I feel my soul through my chest
    grabbing on the back of my shoulders
Clinging on for dear life as it's pulled out,
    removal of molars
      With no novocaine nor laughing gas
    Pain is the experience but I'm not up for the task
Each time a piece is torn my soul screams out
    from my heart
Everything I've known true collapsed,
    falling apart
The me that once was will never return
    Pieces of my soul torn, tossed, and burned

God I followed your call here, I heeded your wish
    But I know not how to swim nor how to fish
I wasn't taught, given the rules everyone else already
    seems to know;
I was tossed in not knowing what role I play in this show

You told me what had to be done
I knew it wouldn't be fun
But for this I was not prepared
The damages too strong they can never be repaired

Surprise, you say, *this is the point*
    My past and my present connecting at a joint
        But no cartilage nor cushion to ease the
        transition
        A place I need all my wit but pain impairs
        cognition
    My greatest lesson I know it is true
        But only if I make it through

You intentionally have me suffering

    Your reasons in the universe far away hovering
Am I meant to stay here? Living in pain, living in fear?

God I followed you here and this is my reward?
My cries for help, for a saviour ignored

Why do you do this? I know there is a reason, by why must
    it be so
    To lose everything dear and parts of my soul
Tearing me up and stripping me down
    Will you rebuild me again and then turn around
                and   break   me
        down once again?

Not sure my heart can handle these ways of men
        The same thing I am trying to escape as
you told me to do
        You told me love shouldn't be this way
but now you do it too

        This is the world of working men, the ones who
make the rules
        The ones you gave powers to, the ones you gave
        the tools

Not a world for the pacifist, the timid, the true
But for the ones who say the right things at the right time
    no matter what they actually do

Integrity doesn't matter and coin is king
A place you need perfect pitch but I can't sing.

My Friend Who Sits on the Edge

You're looking for something my dear friend but what
can it be
          you look to the outside but it's not found in me
               Nor in a man or woman or thing
                       It is in you
               The healing is for you to do

Please find it, I witness you slipping
          My heart is full, I try to do some tipping
               Of the peace I have within, trying to pour
          some in your cup
But you are the one who must choose to sip it up

Please find it, I see it, I know it's there
          You are not alone, but have to be the one who
will care

Honest with your demons, the truth will set you free
          Break those damn chains and let bygones be
Do the work, get treatment, short-term torture is better
than losing it all
          And you are so close to the edge I don't want to
watch you fall

I believe in you, there is pureness and light

Stop running to the darkness, the things that craft the night

My dear friend you sit on the edge
You forget beneath you is ground, you
remain on the ledge
Look around you, wake up, look around, for if you do
You will see there is an entire surface that surrounds,
Beneath you so steady
is the ground.

Be Wary of the Sharks My Love

Paddle out of these waters my love, be cautious as you do
      So determined, *won't get lost*, I know you think
this true

But lost before you did, let the waves steered you away
      You forgot who you are, let the weather your
mind persuade

The billows came, you couldn't stop it, too young and
small back then
      No mother present, nor the help of any men

Just a little seed
      Your heart aching, no filling that need
On your own you ventured out
      Should have been a girl scout
But you weren't, you were in the ocean, out on your own
Life threw you a Tsunami, though you asked for a bone

It hit you with no remorse
      Altering forever, change in life course

Cut and bleeding, hanging on for dear life
      Scared of sharks, scared of strife
Winds and punishing waters left you lost in your boat
      Beat up and frayed, but it still stay afloat

You curled up in a ball in your little canoe
      Not knowing another way or what else to do
You let your mind take you to lands off afar
Someplace out of this ocean someplace beyond the stars

This saved you then, but you got stuck
      It was time to come back, deal with the yuck

You grew up, were strong but believed you still a child
You focused on the Tsunami your thoughts went wild

Uncurled you sat up and looked at the waters ahead
      Two seas in front of you now, but only one I'd
recommend

One direction appeared calm but was the most dangerous
of all
      You knew this river's end was a treacherous
waterfall

But the other river that was meant for you had shock
waves still around
      The same ones that hit you and knocked you to
the ground

You didn't want to deal with those damned beasts
      So you choose the calm river, falsely safe retreat
            A fake a phoney, a real fugazi
You knew but cared not, you longed for some safety

Fake or not it felt so good till you saw what lie before
      No, oh no you can't take anymore
The fall was near your heart began to howl
      You searched for a way back, anything to plough

For you picked up two little birds along the way
In your canoe next you is where they liked to lay
        If you went down they were sure to follow, too
young to fly away
                Suddenly a surge of energy hit you
        To save these birds anything you would do

You used your bare hands bloody in the water
        To get back to the other path and accept the
slaughter
Facing shame, embracing all the tides that would surely
hit you
        You realised you weren't alone you had a crew

                They were far away sure but sent helpful
        currents your direction
Grace and no judgement just pure affection

You made it to land and rested for awhile
Everything would be alright you would find your smile

But as life always does it calls us back to the ocean
        Stay calm and don't be flooded by emotion

Be wary of Sharks as you get back on this journey
They smell you have bled and want to be your attorney
        False representation taking everything you know
to be true

And along it the goodness that's left inside you

Don't be fooled by these sharks as you continue
       Go to your breath and Asana, use your sinew

Be wary of sharks my love. they smell that you've bled
Stay in control, Santa, leader of your own sled.

My Scars Hate the Rain

My scars hate the rain

Lightning cracks shooting pain

Scars shout *the storm is coming,* pounding pours

Pain, a tolerant, must be endured

Pinching of hip, throbbing in joint

Okay rain, you've made your point.

Sounds of the Night Beat in the Day

Once a shout now a whisper that comes and goes at bay
It does not care if I am weak in fact for that it preys
When I am lost it sings its song like whispers in the night
I can't go on I can't be right
It tells me in its taunt
I lay my head and plug my ears squeezing tight my eyes
I hum it's all right hoping it won't recognise my disguise
I thought I killed it many times but learned it can't be killed
It can't be changed never forgotten but at least it can be stilled
Just have to keep going have to remember what slows its rearing head
Smell the flower, blow out the candles
you're safe here in this bed
Now I know I can accept this haunt will never leave
At least I know what to expect this taunting in my dreams

It always comes back but not for long
Stay the course and change the rhythm of most the song
When it shows itself throughout the day
I don't have to let it stay, I don't have to play
I can thank it for its lessons and watch it pass on by,

Fine it says but *I'll be back*
In case then you're feeling more off track
I know I say *I'll see you in my sleep*
　　Ah but not just then it boasts to me, *you see, succumb,*
　　I can't be beat
　　My smile and my words are not what it hoped to hear
　　　　I know you live to stunt the healing heart; I know
　　　　your game the one that thrives on fear

　　　　　　I take a slow breath and long exhale
　　　　It's gone, for now the good fight will
　　prevail
　　　　　　A tinge of doubt in my healing heart
　　　　Reminds me I can yet still fall apart
But off you go, *goodbye* I say
　　Each time I watch you go
　　I know you'll come back unannounced but each time
　　your energy's more low

The sounds of night beat in the day
But for now I sent it away.

Must Fly

I once was a shell wrapped upon myself, scratching to get
    out
My weakness entrapment left me screaming all about

How did this happen? How can it be? I've been here once
    before
The itching the madness beating down my every door
        I escaped once but not for long
 I ran to something different but he sang the same song
I guess I realised but not exactly
      Did I really think he could make me happy?
I must have known the chaos this life choice would
    certainly bring
Yet I must have felt a certain comfort in his humiliating
    sting
The same thing that broke me, the same thing I escaped
      I ran to it actually leapt, for a second take
This one was different, it had an edge I'd never seen
      A level of happiness and physical joy, and he felt
        so damn clean
A carnal love not meant to last
      Just a temporary fix to try to heal my past
The place this would take me I never knew possible
      Beautiful and horrid depths
To escape I knew I would be responsible
Must keep breathing , must keep doing the steps

Sometimes I think I would not do this dance again
I would go back and change the moves, never this life
    would I recommend
Yet something halts me from this notion
        Maybe I was supposed to drink this potion
For this journey carried me here
To a place of knowing that I never knew existed
Maybe I was meant to find it, maybe I would have missed
    it
        Had it not been for the gravel that carried me here
           grinding and spitting me out
             But this land is dry, I must seek the rain,
        escape from this drought
Break this new shell that has been cast
Perhaps heal once and for all from my past

Go to that part of the atmosphere where only butterflies
    dare to go
For this unto me is a life I can and will bestow.

Poem from a Tooth

I am wasting away
> If not pulled soon I will decay

I tried to warn you when you were young
> What life in this world would become

I made it hurt I made it sting
> Tried to show you the obstacles life would bring

I'd give you a fever and make your ears hurt
> Pain I admitted would make you blurt

You would cry and rub at your cheeks
> This would come and go lasting for weeks

Maybe you'd get a little assistance
> But In this world you can't take the path of least
> resistance

The path will hurt and make you cry
> I tried to teach you this but why oh why?

You didn't listen to me;
> I tried to show you but you always expected glee

I warned you no one could understand the crux of your
pain
> But you didn't listen, blocking this from your brain

Life will make you uncomfortable unexpectedly
> You must bare it collectively

You cannot run from or stop pain
> Have to accept it, see what lessons you will gain

For each sharp sting is teaching you something

Stick it out and keep breathing, you'll have something
   worth munching
Like you had to do with me, and I gave you a tool for
chewing
But your perspective is strange, not sure how you're
viewing

Are you punishing me for trying to show you?
         You are breaking my heart, turning me to goo
I guess you couldn't handle the pain life would give
         I know one thing for sure: this is no way to live
Inhaling these chemicals that are making me rot Shopping
      for something that can never be bought
For a life without pain doesn't exists
         Now your insides are like a giant cyst
I am leaving you now, you slowly have killed me
I've been crumbling and rotting during your escape spree
I don't have long left now and I know you won't be far
   behind
         Oh why did this happen, why did you destroy your
            mind
Your soul waits for you too, as you left it long ago
         I'm going to it now, to that little girl that I know
I can't wait to see her
         The purest form, before you turned to a blur
You probably won't even feel me now going
         As your high again, swarms of crack blowing
I am happy to leave this form you have become
         I tried but I failed and now we've turned to scum

I tried to warn you, I really did
But I was just a tooth and you were just a kid.

Old Miser Time

He never slows down no matter how much you plead
>He doesn't bend, doesn't alter no matter how much
>you knead

He is ruthless with his clues
>Doesn't matter if you booze or what path you
>choose

For the runner and vegan may leave at forty-two
>The hustler and the addict seems forever to stay
>and stew

The only thing you can be sure of is he's sneaky and swift
He is the curse but also he's the gift
When you don't want him to he slows
>When you're having fun you don't know where he
>goes

Sometimes you just need him to be fast
>Need him to help you heal, make the pain the past
>Of course then he takes his time
>>But not when you're in your prime
>Oh no then he likes to speed

He cares not what you think he cares not what you need
>Why does he play these games

Taunting us all with false claims
>Do this or do that and I'll give you more
>>But you can never settle that score
>In this game the house always wins

If you're lucky not till your skin thins

But when we lose to him we won't know it till it's done
    Sometimes it seems that life has just begun
The good days gone
The bad seem long

    And who is there to blame
    Time that old miser; curse his name.

Living in the Gray

It is with great sadness that I tell you I live in the gray Try
    as I might to change, I have failed, dismay
I wish I could take the easier road, the one that picks a side
I know it's less lonely and I certainly have tried

Those who pick a side and live in the black
    Know what they know and can't be lead off track
And those who pick the white—eew
    They are quite the crew
So just, so righteous, and so damn wise
    The other side then is easy to despise

But unfortunately I had to stay in the gray
    A place where others like to try and lead you
    astray
It makes people so uncomfortable, it eats at them so
    Throws off the ego, this place that I know
Not the most comfortable but worth the unrest
    This is the suffering to truly progress
Acceptance that there is no wrong or right
This makes a future for our youth far more bright.

Crosshairs

There was a dream that I had when I would play in my
youth
     A vision of two men and me finding my truth
Like an oracle I must have predicted
     Maybe so when I got here I wouldn't be so
conflicted
I would know somehow I was always meant to get here So
strange how it happened, the whys disappear
     But happened it did the crosshairs of my dreams
     Where he's standing there and I'm in between
     One who comes lifts me and inspires new hope
Not like this one who keeps me walking tightrope
     One's a lover not my friend anymore
The other a friend that leaves me wondering more
     One takes care of my calls but shatters my spirit
     The other who's history I'm nowhere near it
Barely knowing him just an instant connection
     That immediate feeling of great affection
Is it wrong to have this when you're already committed?
Perhaps not when the one you're with prefers your heart
pitted
     Perhaps not even if you're happy and the one
you're with is kind
        Perhaps we should share our hearts the
thoughts of our mind
     The problem is the other doesn't like to share

This notion excuses his temper to flare
Even if these feelings are Platonic
The lover has control and anger that is chronic

Will I ever escape it or am I meant to be here
Not getting what I want and staying because of fear
Am I supposed to be happy or
is this part of the deal
A relationship that keeps me constantly
needing to heal?
I could leave him and be no longer in between
But then what would that mean?
I think I need to find out
If only to have friends that make my heart free of doubt
And believe in the goodness of our kind
Not pretending things didn't happen, choosing to be blind
The torment of this relationship always
clawing at my mind
The eyes of the sky are a trick
They get me to trust, then change, making me sick
The other is dark in colour with hair like a bear
But sweet as honey with a soft stare
How did I get here? So strange is this world
Hands that create and hair that is curled
To hands too rough
and words not enough
But if it weren't for these crosshairs
I would have no hope
If I have to be tortured at least one throws me a rope

This one may toss me in the ocean,
      flaring out my arms
But the other lets me know not all men seek to harm.

Pack Animals

Profound wisdom overshadowed by the need to feel
connected
    People accepting of our dying being neglected
Family's estranged
    Yelling people enraged
They cling so tight to a side
    Choosing this people have died
Why do they feel they need to pick
    The illusion it makes their house made of brick
    When in fact that choice alone is like picking straw
    And makes the soil beneath them weak and raw
How can they not see why history continues to be
repeated?
    We keep doing the same things over and over,
    admission of this deleted
Since when is it ever a good idea to only see one side of
the story?
    Wiser men than me keep preaching this glory
    When is life ever black or white?
    Why is the grey area such a plight?
    How has a new party in the middle not succeeded
    by now?
They can never win that's how
    You see I have decided something
    That people feel more comfortable judging
They don't want to admit there is no right answer

Like tobacco companies don't
want to stop cancer
If they do this you see they will feel unstable
It would be like walking life on a cable
I know because I climb that tree
And when it gets tough there is no one near to
help me
It's isolating and confusing
Branches hit you, your heart takes a bruising
But from this dark journey of deep
understanding and compassion
Come the only true solution I can ration
The only long-term game means we must sit in it
Cannot retreat, cannot quit; we have to be brave
and channel our wit
To be okay with things not being okay
To admit that life is better seeing the grey.

Devil's Advocate

Push those feelings down darling
    Sweep them under the rug
        There's no point in quarrelling
            Make-up, go give a hug

When I'm upset you'd better heed
    But when you are it's selfish greed
        If I tell you to you better fight
        Do what I say for I am always right
Your feelings—I'll always give you the opposing view
    For feelings I can always misconstrue
You never can win
So crawl out of your skin

I am always here telling you to be happy when you tear
Or knock you down when you're feeling happy
    You think your patient I think you should be
    snappy

The advocate of devils
    I tell you to keep it simple but add many levels
Don't be too happy or sure
    It make us uncomfortable, those of us who never
expect more
    When you do good don't brag
Feeling too good about yourself is a drag

If you know something someone else always
        knows it better
You shouldn't read that newsletter
                        Read this instead
Still feel different? Oh you just misunderstood
        With me I can I always find a should
Water you will always have to tread
        Torture of the devil's advocate can always be felt
But it could be worse: a harder hand could always be dealt.

Don't Marry Men Whose Mothers Don't Love Them

Don't marry men whose mothers don't love them
Lest you be chewed up like a piece of gum
      I'm telling you don't do it
      Doesn't matter how good your spirit
You think he's innocent will appreciate you more
Instead he'll be trying to settle a score
      He needs constant attention strange reassurance
      Arguing will be a regular occurrence
Or he'll demand constant attention
You'll be the point of his focus his constant obsession
      He'll always be trying you see
      Playing out his childhood plea
The one that shouts for a time out
The one that says hold me when I pout
      The one that says do more, no do less
      Do a handstand, now a cartwheel, anything to
         impress
You will always be trying and always failing
He will always be unhappy and always be wailing
      There is a hole you see that you can't fill
      But your soul indeed he will try to kill

So run away from him, darling, as fast as you can
And please, never marry that kind of man.

Burning of Coal

Children keep people together long after they should have
    parted
So the journey where it should end just gets started
       The baby's so pure and so clean
           You can pretend and think you can change
            scene
Perhaps they do change it, at least for a moment
       But that element's always there, that key
        component
The thing you can't ignore, at least not forever
       The thing that creeps up, the thing that severs
          Instead of learning and moving on
       You look at your child and sing a song
You put up with the nonsense and the games
           Wishing you could be happy with their
           parent but hating the claims
       The claims that this person takes on your soul
It's more than your time, a burning of coal
       That slowly singes your dreams
          Howling inside: 'get out 'it screams
            You're meant to think big, to be
             supported when you grieve
      Not judged and alone and them turning to leave
        Not this person you once trusted
That's long since gone, a pipe that has rusted
      Only unlike pipes you can never fully return

To that hope that sparkle for its
caution you learn
Don't trust them enough to be happy but
too scared to retreat
For at least you know what is on this dark street
If you turn and run down another, who knows what lies
there
Plus there's a child, so delicate so rare
Looking to Mommy and Daddy connected to both
Already confused by this process of growth

Apart does it sever a bond that they have?
A circle once whole now seems halved
Some say no
They wished it happened long
ago
Another forever changed
Innocents tousled rearranged
What to do, no one knows
So you pause in the midst of throes
Hoping for answers while your child grows.

Blocked Your Phone

The spot in my heart where love was planted has rotted and
    died
It cannot be mended, nor replaced, too many tears it's cried
Tears fell down with no remorse, your action to blame
    drowning the land till nothing remained
        but mouldy remnants of what we became

You said you couldn't go back, no not ever, but you did,
    many times, not just my heart this time that you
    severed
I tried to save you and pull you back
        Doing more and more picking up the slack
Nothing I could do; I learned the hard way it's true
        Could change your demons your warped sense of
        view
The glasses you wear are clouded with darkness so black
        Your perspective stings: a shocking smack
            I'm always surprised but why I know not
              I know how it is this is our plot
                This is you
            It's what you do
      I guess my dreamer's heart always had hope
Wishing those glasses would turn telescope
      Seeing the big picture, seeing the good
          The cosmos, the stars how I wished you
          would

But you didn't, you coward, I should have
known you could

You could go back to the darkness
You are no role model, you are no Marcus
    For Aurelius didn't hide behind cowardly ways
    He took accountability for the games he played
       This life is ours our actions our own
You've no one to blame but you when you lie there alone
    Repeated slamming with words and more
Peaceful days and a childhood you turned to war

But I don't have to stay, not any longer
    No more of my life will I squander
       So as I set forth on a journey of
       conservation
          I am taking back my power, I am
    changing this station
I leave you to your land to deal with as you please
          I am no longer yours whose juice
          you get to squeeze
The ache of being drained to water your dessert of a heart
    No longer my cross to bear, I get a new start
          I am happy to leave before my
          soil turns to ash and dust
       My secrets and heart I share no more, for
    you lost my trust

So keep your dry land with no foliage and watch the storms
    that roam
Just don't call me because I've blocked your phone.

Alone

You say you feel alone but I'm sitting right here
    Saying you don't have to worry, telling you not to
        fear
Alone is when you walk away and I'm sobbing all night
Alone is when I'm hurting and you decide to start a fight
    Alone is when you have no one to trust and no one
        to lean on
        Alone is when you reach out and
        realise they're gone

    Spilling of guts unbearable vulnerability
    Met with disgust, anger, and humility
A longing so painful and met with no care
A warning, a siren, a loud-sounding flare
    That doesn't even make you blink
    You just keep doing the same thing and you think
        That I'll always be here trying to
        make your life better
But I won't any more; didn't you get my letter?

Alone is when you want to quarrel but I can't be found
Alone is what you are now cause I'm not around.

I Gave up a lot of Freedom to be Free

I gave up a lot of freedom to be free
      But the legal systems lets his hand still have a
grip on me

I gave up my rights, or so I was told
      Those years ago when I said to have and to hold

I didn't know what for worse would mean
        I was too young, too damn green

      Seventeen years old when I fell in love
Not knowing he would always want to hover above
      Keep me pinned to the floors
        Close me behind his wealthy doors
If I tried to dance , he'd change the song
      Despite the trip to France, these trenches of
marriage I did not to belong

Gruelling work, army crawling my way out
      But this damn GPS keeps putting me on re-route

Family law in the south
      Mine as well be a bad word
        Go wash out your mouth
      Moldy as a cheese curd

Infected and wrong on so many levels
       I couldn't care less, I am now part of the rebels

I will not be broken by judgments of others
I will stand in my truth as survivor, an abused mother

An leave this man with power and pull
       And let my heart shine and be full

Yes I gave up my freedom to be free
       But one thing they can never take from me

My soul, my purpose, and my truth
       I don't have to live in mistakes of my youth

I will move on and I will soar over head
       Letting them think they have won instead

I choose to lose the battle so my soul can win the war
       And for that, the world I am able to offer more

Despite the suffering, I have more glee
       Than with him I could ever see

Energy and sharing of tea,
       With all these peaceful warriors beside me

Now that my head in above the surface
     The sight of him no longer makes me nervous

Yes, material and rights, and preservation of ego,
                    I gave up
     And I'd do it all again, this agonising breakup

I gave up a lot of freedom to be free
     But my soul can never be taken away from me.

Take 3

The Petal

All things should be so beautiful, that is the goal
    The truth of existence, the language of soul

    Even as it wilts before us the petal finds grace
    Appreciates what is and embraces this place

The sweet scent of life with all the flaws and beauty
Enjoyment it adds before it goes, fulfilling its duty

    The petal is soft and lands gently before it drifts
Decomposing with meaning, life's purpose not missed.

Religion

I have vision as it so seems
        that the religion of you and the religion of me
          brings only peace in my dreams
        It doesn't know certainty of wrong or right
A sounding board perhaps to keep sight of the light
           Not just for the poor or wealthy or daft
        Not do this and do that and life throws you a raft
      Just some tools to be taken and put in your pack
          Leave the sharp and extreme or you'll
          puncture your sack

If ritual so suits you, then ritual you may
           Just be careful when the storm
            comes to not be at bay
     For the wind's ever shifting
      Tide's ever strong
           Just when you think you got it
             You'll be proven wrong
You can't see the ending from the beginning
          But you can learn the lessons
          instead of just spinning

But what if we don't and just keep crusading along?
         Then perhaps it's all for nought
      Perhaps peace isn't to be found amongst this lot
Perhaps we'll never learn—perhaps it doesn't matter

The protests, the murders, the
pandemonium or the latter
No war, no virus, no miracle, no cure
Everyone isolating, are we that insecure
The sick left alone—no visitors please
Who's judge and jury of what makes someone impure
Not offended? okay what about the
genocide disease
Since the beginning of recorded history
this plagues our lands
No pharaoh, nor king, nor German can bury this
history in sands
History of the great Russian Czar
Sudan, Iraq, Syria, the Rohingya and CAR
Rwanda , Cambodia, Nigeria, to name a recent few
Not to mention our Native history becoming the
great red, white, and blue

The depths of this quickly go too far
So let's cut to the chase
It's dark and it's dreary
And here is a theory:
If we want to save the human race
Let's learn from the past
Not keep making the same mistakes
Hold tight or let go of
every religion and
obstacle you know
If it doesn't shout amity

Then it doesn't serve humanity
Drop your guard and breathe deeply in and out
Hold hands and comfort and wander about
Keeping loving, keeping learning, and keep it moving
Something new is about something worth improving.

Brooms of Cinnamon

Brooms of cinnamon standing pleasantly by each grocery
    door
        A mother of youth takes two more
She brings them home to her giddy kin
The smell means candy and bringing up the holiday bin

Hot apple cider and crunching of fall leaves
        Deciding a costume and breaking out long sleeves
The orange gooey beast giving slimy seeds
        Rinsed, dried and cooked: a salty treat it breeds
Some like the crunch of the shedded leaves from the trees
        Others find comfort in the crisp fall breeze
            Retreating in a sweater
        And sending of fall letters
Will the light be on? If so ring the bell

But this year he doesn't like that smell
        It stops him in his tracks when he entered the
        grocery store
        He pictures lying down, right there on the floor
His wife always bought those this time of year
        He loved coming home to them, the memory
        brings a tear
The house would smell of cinnamon
        All the treats lying about; one had to have
        discipline

Begonias and pumpkins lined the entry
> Apple bread mixed with pumpkin, the flavours are
> quite complementary

She'd put on the big witches hat on the thirty-first
> Tell the children the house had a curse

You must take at least four candies to break this awful spell
> At least that is what she use to say when the
> children rang the bell

But this year there would be no answer
> His wife had died defeated by cancer

He left the cart where he stood, empty and alone
> And turned and walked out, his hair over grown

No he wouldn't turn the lights on this year after all
He would just go home and into bed he'd crawl.

Candy Apple Cheeks

Candy apple cheeks round like a plumb
A rose wrapped around stem, the sucking of
thumb
Plump little lips that look like their painted
Lighting up of eyes from a heart that's untainted
Baby hairs soft as feathers that curl at the end
Thick long lashes of black that bend
For the crying eyes to mend
A soft snuggly bear I retrieve
Tiny little nose like the button on sleeve
Bitsy fingers grab soft bear toy with relief
In the circling of planets this moment is brief
But for me my life purpose is in this moment
Every ounce of the universe and every component
This porcelain skin doll
Needs me to grow tall
Yet still I need her more
How my heart ever beat before I'm unsure

Her smile and big cheek flop down on my shoulder
My heart grows bigger each time that I hold her
Bath times filled with bubbles and singing of song
Knowing for once I'm just where I belong
Mashing of food that is green, orange and yellow
Making animal shapes out of jello
Baby powder and playing peek-a-boo

Now Velcro but later teaching the tying of shoe
Drooling on my chest as she sleeps so deep
These moments so precious making me weep
                    They go by so fast before
            you know it they're gone
                    The stretching of little arms and a
                    scrunchy little yawn
        Learning to crawl and pull herself up
To walking and running and chasing the pup
            So much beauty from her view I try to capture
                Each moment a whole new chapter
                    Filling pages in my book
Time passes so quickly now that old crook;
I ask him to slow down so I don't miss the moment
        But time's not my friend he's my opponent
                    Must write it down, must take
                    these pictures
                    Must stay in the moment and read
                    wise scriptures
So I can remember these days and feel this same fondness
        Take these full breaths and hold on to this
        calmness
                Knowing I'm right where I need to be and
                complete
        For these little clean, soft feet
Are counting on me to show them the way
                    To teach them to catch and teach
                    them to play
What better gift I can offer her but what she showed me

To be in each moment to meet it with glee?
For it goes by so fast you don't want to miss
Each small moment, each little kiss
Appreciate the day and place that you're in
Be mindful and remember the smell of baby skin
So innocent so mindful and so delighted
The elements of life before you being cited
In one little moment that makes up the whole thing
To be in each moment, the giving of wing

Will free you from the ground, you'll soar to new heights
Connection in time and great insights

So kiss those baby feet and see how they wander
And dazzle and learn and marvel at thunder.

Someplace Beautiful

Take me someplace beautiful that's far away from here
                    Where the goldfinch are singing
            and there's no more fear
Riding with no saddle, swimming with no cloth
            Hair that doesn't tangle, butterfly kissing moth
A flat in historical setting, drawings on the ground
            Books stacked for nightstands and paintbrushes
            all around
Soft curls of brown that wrap around my finger
            Candles burning out leaving smells that linger
                        Softly in the air
            Like the warmth of a prayer
            Showering together sharing same sink
Fights they just don't happen, safely having drink
                    Days so simple full of so much bliss
            Moments seem to last never going amiss
Walk down to the baker, a coffee and croissant
            Anything with you is all I ever want
Still holding hands and arms around my waist
            This spot you hold in mine can never be replaced
            I'd laugh with you in a flat any day of the week
            Than go back to that mansion ever so bleak
You kiss my back so perfectly as steady as they come
            Rhythm of our hearts a perfect beating drum
I knew it when I saw you, a calmness planted inside
            But fear held me back, the shortcomings of pride

I'd go back and release if I knew it'd bring me there
    If I knew you waited I'd freed the snare
        Long ago—so much time I
        wasted
           Sacred time can never be
           recreated
I tried to stick it out, so much force and sweat
        To this day I have so much
        lingering regret
    If I only knew, if I wasn't so blind
    If I could have freed myself, had a stronger mind
But I didn't and can't change the course
    Just be here now, live freely no remorse
A blink and his voice brings me back to the now
    I'm not free yet, need to be—but how?
Oh take me there please
    Give strength to these wings
        The freedom from cultural rings and other
        material things
        The courage to say I deserve to soar
The cage of his grip holding me back no more

Oh take me someplace beautiful that's far away from here
    Where the goldfinch are singing and there's no
    more fear
Spilt milk that doesn't matter
    Hearts that never shatter
        Pages of books and fingers that draw
No guards standing by, freezing now thaw.

Mystic Rhyme

It flows like a river till it hits the ground
It trickles softly, a tranquil sound
So cool yet warm at the same time
Bodies moving, mystic rhyme
Grazing lips, arms intertwined
This type of ecstasy makes us blind
A few moments of pure bliss
A tender touch, a gentle kiss
All I need, hearts amiss
A movement so natural and so pure
Where I belong here I'm sure
In these arms every night
Letting littles go, never fight
My stomachs deepest sensations twirl
Moving of fluids, a cosmic whirl
Sweet sweat smearing, on and across
I am on top and he is my boss
Guide with your hands my love
Freedom to fly, wings on dove
Peaceful excitement, organs that hum
Silk fabrics breeze by White clouds in the sky
He pulls me back to him retraction of flower
His arms wrap around, I let go of my power
Just hold me, a swaddle, comfort so dear
Feeling of love, a single happy tear
His finger traces along down my back

The bonding of bodies, a covenant, a pack
The artist with brush, the canvas is I
Whatever he needs, I will be by
For now it is closeness and changing of fluid
An arrow struck, the work of Cupid.

Squeezing of Clay

My last supper is coming but how will it land
> for my work never seems to go as planned

Enjoy the process is what they say to do
> The torment every artist must hide ensues

Pretend it's all fun, daydreams and glory
> But that is not this artist's story
> Sometimes sure, but it's not an endless parade

More like I'm frantic, cleaning up messes like a maid
> A mess my mind creates as it tortures itself
> A list of things to do: it's Santa I'm elf

Make, create, figure this out
The world is a wreck, don't fumble about

I think I landed on the wrong planet, got lost in the stars
> Landed in this place with hookers and bars

With orphans and war and pimps and starvation
> The only way I'll make it is to keep at creation

No words can describe the boiling water I hold
> Trying to fit in a world with a mould

Of unspoken rules and laws even worse
> Escape in my work, escape to verse

A slow emptying of hot water spilling out of my brain The
> steeping of tea, release like a drain

The work is all I have at the end of the day
> No therapist nor lover can help my dismay

Not enough time to drain all this madness
      Not enough paint not enough canvas
      So writing I do with urgency and fervour
      The orders keep coming and I am the server
What will it be today?
Let the work shape me, squeezing of clay.

Colours of Pigment

Colours of pigment bleed gracefully on canvas
    With right placement a cure for sadness
So soft are his strokes from gentle bristle
    My lines are harsh stem prickles like thistle
The colours dart your eye around the page like magnets
    The eye knows not just enjoys these tactics

Donatello, Da Vinici, Michelangelo, Degas…
    He's Turner and La Tour while I petite bourgeois
Rembrandt, Monet, Botticelli
    Excitement upon viewing swirls in belly
Renoir, Van Gogh, and Rafael
    Works ensured to cast mystic spell
They draw you in with timeless vigour
Delectation when talent meets perseverance and rigour

I thank them all for these gifts, can't try to compete
    Yet still back to my pencil and brush I retreat.

New Moon

Energy swirls again, it's a new moon
Some of us go werewolf while others may bloom
The ocean's pull gets stronger
Sometimes things feel longer
Then they actually are
The road may seem long the journey far
Or perhaps it feels an exciting awakening
An opportunity for change yours for the taking

The path is yours no one else knows how it feels
We all are just here often spinning our wheels
Disciples of growth this clan came together
Hummingbirds flying, the flapping of feather
Those who want to fly not in just one direction
The guidance we need, a smart confession
The rotation of planet the turning of tides
Ancient text and elements being our guides
Transcend down a path to wherever it will lead
The posture is the practice, the mat is our creed
Keep going, don't stop for the second you do
You'll fall back into patterns
forget what you knew
Life is vast meditation for those who choose wisely
A glow in the darkness, the star shining brightly

So werewolf or flower just tune in

Be happy and take the path with a grin
For this life experience is short anything can happen
Tomorrow not promised, yesterday already gone
Every breath a new opportunity, the rising of dawn.

Let Go

How scary to let go yet so freeing
    For beauty we are not seeing
When we cling so tight to our demands
    We hear not peaceful commands
Sometimes hard and scary at best
    Life asks us to trust and let go of the rest
But what if I lose when I let go? I want to know the ending
    of this show
But that's not part of the deal
    Not knowing is what makes us real
    I want to do better I want to heal
        How bad do you want it? Life asks of me
    Are you willing to let go, to let things be?
Only then if you try it you will see
    What life really has in store for you
        Your authentic purpose the
        magic the true

I've felt it before the freedom it brings
    This is the thing that lifts birds wings
A trust and knowing that life has you covered
    If you're brave enough to go to the undiscovered
    Release and let go, surrender to the abyss
        The only way to find divine bliss

That peace that you feel when you
connect with another dimension
The one that's there when you let
go and pay attention
So pure and so strange when you feel this
The brush of pureness our souls first kiss.

Canoe

I am tired of this road dear Lord you want me to take
      It's rough and rocky, I believe I may break
I am not scared or frightened, my ego has left me
      I trust you and know this path I must agree
But I'm tired and the end of the trail I can no longer see

      I know I agreed to this path long before birth
But I'm tired dear lord as I'm stuck here on Earth

I don't know your reasons though I know they are there
      I know the final act you cannot share
I accept it, I surrendered, I know there is a reason
But this time is different, a new changing of a season

No ego, nor trauma, no emotions run my choice
      As I whisper to you, I know you hear my voice
      I can't take another step, I can't even see the end
I know there is one but my knees will not bend
      They know they have to keep moving,
                      there's nothing else to do
      Your voice comes to me and tells me,
    then hop into my canoe

I look left and I see it, a river is there
      The water moves not, the canoe stable as
    if floating on air
      Steady and strong but made of soft wood
I listen to you and walk to it, not knowing I could
      I climb in your canoe and lie flat on my back
Palms facing up, accepting you have all I lack

      You can see the bigger play

You know the dawn before we even start one day
I close my eyes, they are oh so tired
I feel exposed but guided, my tiredness has not expired

But I know I cannot yet retire
Yet here now safe in your canoe
I trust your warmth will help me do what I must do.

Nobody Complains of Pooping

Nobody complains of pooping—Could you even imagine?
Ah can you believe I had to poop today?!
  That would be the end, the relationship assassin
We would surely be crazy, outcast and insane
    For accepting what we must do as humans must be
      ingrain
    We can't think about it, can't hyper-focus
    We know it is coming for the rest our lives, our
      human locus
Complaining about it would cause undue sadness
    For there is nothing to change it, to think so is
      madness
    Who on earth would waste time thinking about
      such a thing?
    Yet the weather, the traffic, the "news", these are
      acceptable complaints to bring
We accept we must poop, it's just the shitty part of life
    Yet all the other normal discomforts we create so
      much strife
      We suffer more each time we complain
We call ourselves intelligent animals using so much of our
  brain
    But we haven't learned by now suffering is all part
      of the game?
      We increase it by harping and acting like
      it should be something else

Our pants keep falling down and we refuse to put on belts
Haven't learned by now that the weather does what
it wants
Surprised at traffic and waits at restaurants
Somehow shocking every time at this
repetitive the news
which is just one side, just a version
intended to confuse
Just a sliver of life and discomforting recursion
The ones we shouldn't give energy to and usually can't
change
Are the ones that have become acceptable to plant
in our grange
Spoiler alert: suffering is inevitable and we all must die
We all get sick and no one really knows why
Our mothers leave us too soon
And the weather's always shifting, there's always
a new moon
Until of course there isn't because everything must shift
Accept and adjust or create a bigger rift
You can't stop the boat from shaking as the waves hit the
sides
But you can keep yourself grounded and have
grace with the tides
Don't panic when it happens; you're smart
and prepared
Ride the wave and stay rooted and your
boat will be spared

No extra waves did you create by freaking out and making
  your boat rock even more
      You dealt with the ones that came and
      drifted ashore
So many around freaking out in their boat, *It's rocking so*
  make it rock more!
      this strange acceptable life abuse
But that's not you,
   no you know better
   You don't complain of pooping and you don't
   complain of weather.

The Road Less Travelled

Follow your heart and go the route of compassion
>Even when you think you can't and think you have
>>to ration

Even if it is the road less travelled
>Even if it is bumpy, even if its gravelled

For flying against the wind at slow pace
>Is better than jetting the wrong way, for life is not
>>a race

It's also not a marathon or sprint or joke or game
>It is not in the followers or how much stuff you
>>can claim

Life is in the breath—this perfect little gift
So though the journey may alter, change, and shift
>Remember your breath and whatever you do don't
>>get lost adrift

Even if it's hard, even if it makes others feel unravelled
>Follow your heart and go the route of compassion,
>>even if it is the road less travelled.

A Christmas Wish

Christmas is coming, it's just around the bend
One thing I sit thinking is what next year we may lend

Will we look back smiling knowing we lived each day
with this spirit in mind?
Will we spend our time sharing without multitasking?
Try it—you may just end up laughing

Will we soften a heart with love, looking past the villain
enabling us to discover the truth?
Will we spend time with the neglected and cherish the
youth?
Will we make our commitment even when circumstance
tries to tell us it can wait?
Will you give someone a chance and discover something
great?
Will we read to a child—this child could be you?
Oh I am so thinking of all the things we could do
If we took the time to look at ourselves and each other
The way a baby does to its mother
If we share instead of hoard, expose instead of isolate
And see what we can give instead of what we can take
Enjoy the little things that bring a smile
And take time to visit your innocent inner child
Now is our time to be kinder and greater
Our time is right now it is not later

We leave footprints everywhere we go
Let's look back on them and be happy we did so.

Sleep Ever So Sweet

I danced with devils and loved monsters, so villains haunt
my dreams
> They mock me in my head saying things aren't as
they seem

> > For with the sun
> > > I don't succumb,
> > > > to these monsters anymore
> > > I've done the work put in the healing, so
> > monsters I no longer wish to endure

But when the sun is hidden away and my eyes attempt to
rest
> These demons know I cannot fight and put my
efforts to the test

They attack my mind I cannot see
> Until they have already gotten in front of me
> > But in his arms laying on his chest
> My mind is finally able to rest
These demons know they have no power
> This man's love washing over me, steam
from hot shower
> Relaxing my nerves and cleansing my soul
His hands on my body, reactions can't control

So strong with skin so soft

a shack an apartment or a loft
On land one day perhaps
But if the time is long since past
And those dreams we never do see

I will not care
My heart will not despair
As long as he's by my side
As long as we're never blindfolded by pride
As long as *I love you* never feels like repeat
And the sleep, oh the sleep, is ever so sweet.

Sweep Me Off My Feet

Pitter patter, horses, tattoos on skin

Making out to Radcliffe, Two hour talks feel like they just begin

Muscles and fragrance, hands on my head

Bend me over gently, the side of bed

Give me time not rushing

His question have me blushing

Not sure my replies

Too busy staring in those eyes

Watch him moving can't seem to get enough

Tender is his touch, not gentle not rough

The goal is living, alive as can be

No more alive than you inside of me

You make this beautiful instead of ugly

Oxytocin release you say when you're cuddly

Not sure where it will go

    Should we be taking it slow

        Perhaps, but that's not our MO

        Jump in we do, and why not

      Life is short, this is our time slot

Perhaps it will be brief perhaps it will be long

        You're showing me new music
    introducing a new song

So take me where I am, broken yet complete

Spread my legs and sweep me off my feet.

Letter to my Lover

You came to my life that day twenty-twenty-two
        I had just decided to stop putting energy
    in folks who make me blue
That day, a Wednesday , I remember it 'cause
    I was coming off some bullshit, that I was
        First-time as a student at that class
Sam had just taught Power yoga and kicked my ass
    Talking to two woman Margret and another
        They were asking me about my woes of
    trying to divorce as a mother
        A friendly hello you got from me, as you
    walked towards the lockers
Unexpected reply from you drove me happily bonkers

That day it started a little cloudy
    In 24 hours you'd give up something, later you'd
tell me about it proudly
        Now you got me letting down
    my walls, dear God
        Making me feel so special and
    strong though you know I'm so flawed
    Tryin to make me fall in love?
Have me thinking of stars and believing in things above

I want to write this letter, documents of you
    Some parts might not make sense, my thoughts
like a zoo

The cages always left open
You have found me in pieces, better yet broken
With you I feel like it was all for a reason
Everything has its window, everything has its season

Some may not be so pleasant

Hopefully it all feels like a present

I want to document this time thoughts and observation

Something special has
happened, changing of vibration

Take some as they are passing of thoughts

One second in my brain
as many thoughts as spots

Scattered across a Dalmatian

Clouds across the sky
my minds creation

Inspiring's, time spent with you

Admiring of morning dew

Gracing your favourite flower

Perhaps some things that sour

Hopefully more of the former

But this is real not the performer

Take to heart the good

Leave the rest where you should

Critiques be taken small, grain of salt

It is better to write and
let out than lock in the vault

I hold back nothing except all I
cannot grasp to release

I write this for you, perhaps for me,

in hopes someday your heart it will appease.

Sleep in the Nude

Breeze and the Sun
  Something has just begun
    I talk, you listen
  Your eyes don't shine they glisten
You talk, I marvel, so much you're not saying
  Trust and honesty it's what I've been praying

Bringer of light, a raven a wing
  Perhaps I'm a queen, perhaps your my king

Curiosity and impulse mixed with comfort
  Compassion first response absent is retort

Some people make you feel more like yourself
They give you that feeling the one you forgot you felt

The silence feels filled not empty in the least
  Just sitting in their presents a comfort and ease

If you find them please take my advice
  Don't think twice just roll the dice
  Kiss him goodbye like he's going to war
    Not just like he's walking out the door
Hold him tight and show him you care
  Life's too short not a moment to spare

So pick me up and place me on your tailgate
　　　　Look at me like we're on our first date

　　　　Talk to me about music and food and
　　play my favourite song
I'll put that leopard on, your favourite thong
　　And lick you like you're my lifeline
I'll play the drunk tonight, you'll be the wine
　　Love is pure, nothing about it crude
　　　　　The space we were suppose to
　　live, before sex got skewed
　　Manipulated for power and control
Not for the audacious, the seekers of soul
　　Shame and judgement has no space for the living
I'll live to the fullest won't ask for forgiving

　　I'll kiss him goodbye like he's heading to war
And spend my time loving not shopping in the store

　　I'll drink that IPA on the tailgate of his car
And sleep in the open where I attempt to count each star

He'll talk to me about music and food
　　And when we're together we'll sleep in the nude.

Tread Softly Sweet Tommy

Wood beneath your feet has rotted
   though surface looks sure
  Confident your footing,
    intentions pure
  But it all means not
One misstep, too hard, too fast, touch the wrong spot
   And the wood that's beneath you shatters,
   falls apart
  There will be no turning back no grace for you
    Unfairness? it's true
Beauty of fallen grace called you to her
  Fogging your judgement vision's a blur
Now you found yourself in the middle crossing her fall
  Do you dare to keep going? Do you even recall?
She whispered her warning when you took your first step
  Beware to cross trees that have fallen and wept
Even the strongest of trees start to decay
  Ones you love that have fallen quickly go away
One wrong word one misstep it's not fair this is true
  but you know this truth of life don't make me teach
  it to you
Tread softly sweet Tommy
  though this branch seems stable
Pressure just slightly too much
  and it will snap like a cable
For she's pretty its true and tempting nonetheless

But test her you'll find the insides broken, a mess
She fragile and frail, though appears to be stable
Her heart is a tightrope, walk it like a cable

Tread softly sweet Tommy, please I must recommend
If you want to keep your footing and walk her to the end.

Excerpts

A blip in the system, some ramblings, some spilling
>The chaos of this mind, sort through the
>mayhem if you're willing
>Perhaps you'll find a mirror reflecting to yourself
>>Perhaps you'll put it up to collect dust on your
>>bookshelf

If anger is stirred when you read
>A good indication it's reflection you need

So proceed if you must to the glitch in the system
Bringing hopefully some thought-provoked wisdom.

Song For My Child

If you find yourself feeling broken and alone
　　　If you find yourself not wanting to pick up when
　　　　　it's me on the phone
Know—it was me, it was me, it wasn't you, wasn't you
　　　When life blows at you
　　　　　　　And you don't know what you're
　　　　　　　　supposed to do
　　　When life beats you down
And I'm nowhere around
　　　When all that is rough
　　　　　Feels like too much
Know—It was me, it was me, it wasn't you, wasn't you

　　　　　If all that is wrong in me
　　　　　　　　Feels like it's wrong with you
　　　　　If all that's in me
　　　Dims the light that you see
　　　　　If all your thoughts feel stuck
　　　Sifting through that muck
Know—It was me, it was me, it wasn't you wasn't you

It was me; it was me, it wasn't you, wasn't you

Those times you didn't know why
　　　Those times you just stood there and cried
　　　　　Those times you feel you failed

Those times you stood and wailed
Those times you felt no one cared
Know—It was me; it was me, it wasn't you, wasn't you. It
was me, it was me, it wasn't you, wasn't you

All that was broke in your life
All that nameless strife
All that was lost
Your innocence paid the cost
All the negative thoughts
Steady like a trot
Know—It was me, it was me, it wasn't you, wasn't you. It
was me, it was me
Know that I tried and I failed
Know that my love still prevailed
Sometimes I didn't try
Sometimes I left and cry
Knowing I let you down
Falling to the ground
Know that I hurt and I blamed
Know that I yelled and I shamed
It was me; it was me, it wasn't you, wasn't you. It was me,
it was me, it wasn't you, wasn't you

I hope that you know
All that was *good* in my life
All that is *good* in your life
All that was *kind*
All that was *bold*

All that in mind
You melted away my cold—

That was you, it was you
That wasn't me, wasn't me
The good that I have
The good that you saw
A mirror of you shining through me

That was you, it was you. That wasn't me, wasn't me. That
was you, it was you.

Don't Lie

I've been writing to you, keeping to myself
    Books sit collecting dust on the shelf
I remain steady wondering what will be
        Just waiting for the universe to sling shot
        you back to me
    I want to be your Helen of Troy
        Never enough never to cloy
When you come back please no ties
    And anything oh anything but lies
    My heart would break more at the sound of that
Than anything oh anything else you could have spat
    For lies I cannot do
        No matter how many promises, good
        things that you spew
Please just be honest
    If there is one thing it is this you must promise
        Dark and ugly, shameful at times
        That I can handle
    Hardships and trials, even a scandal
Just don't lie about it ever
    For one single lie this bond will sever
So do what you do, in Austin, in Texas
    Just keep us united, don't cut our plexus.

Stuck in a Moment

Stuck in a moment, high on a feeling
        Let my heart open again now there's no
        chance of healing
Was actually thinking this time, yet still got lost
        Was trying to follow the map at any cost

His eyes took me out to a tropical sea
        No roads, no turns, just bliss for me
            Needed to stay grounded, follow my path
        But he smiles and instead I hop on his raft

One damn smile one soft conversation
        That's all it took, little temptation
        I hopped on no questions, trusting the feeling
            Fletcher song plays, *I'm still healing*
        His eyes the ocean euphoria appealing
            Forgot my mission averted my task
Didn't even check for life vests, didn't even ask

Love is blind, such old truth
        I have it now sure but what good is it here
When you follow those eyes and don't know how to steer
        Coming in so fast, swooped me quick
        Is it all just an illusion all just a trick
The waves carry me out, heart on the sea
Bag in my cup, warm spot of tea

My soul ignited like nothing before
What point is there to stop, closing of door
I'm already hooked, my heroine my crack
Can't let it go I'll do anything for his smack

My souls on fire purpose ignited
The interment of souls united
For this moment in time okay I jumped in
I'll deal with the consequence
later now watch my heart spin
I'll enjoy every moment
For as long as I hold it
For I'm stuck in a moment, high on a feeling
And he's the only thing about my world right now that's
appealing.

Writing You Love Letters

Writing you love letters, waiting for life to bring you back
    to where I am
        Trying hard to be patient, but damn
                Not sure that I can
Think you forgot about me
        Maybe I got carried away, lost at sea
Perhaps the feelings were my side alone
            I really didn't think so but you haven't
                picked up the phone
            Last was me who contacted you
        You left, to where I have no clue
Perhaps in her arms back in love you fell
        Perhaps I hold not your heart's spell
            Perhaps I imagined it all
        The connection the fire the giant fall
            Intertwined instantly, love at first sight
Maybe you're just my muse, something to write

        Disturbing this notion, can't stand the thought
            No he was mine, that notion I bought
        Perhaps he was normal, a clever one sure
Perhaps my bay wasn't only his allure
        Without its offering nothing to come back to
            An ache in the chest if this be true

Perhaps I got played
Another hope lost, not one stayed.

Free Verse

Life's Answers

The key to life, the trick, the secret
Make a mistake but don't keep repeating it
I know this rule see and try to live this code
But my mind is so sly and so quick
It convinces me to do the repeated
A place it can rest and not have to work
You see it wants to be on constant vacation
Resting on a hammock sipping a drink
It panics when placed with too many new challenges
Be wary of minds like this: there is something there they
    don't want to share
A lamp with a genie, a drink that makes you tall or cracker
    that makes you small
A nightingale or goldfinch or rare birds going extinct
A formula, an answer it doesn't want to share
For when it does it knows it can never go back to its
    comforts
It's scary for a brain, it knows things, see
It knows it will be asked more and more and never be
    allowed to go back to the simple way it was before
So the key to life, the trick, the secret
Train your mind to be your servant instead of your master
Only then will you really know the secret, life's greatest
    answers.

Not Bored

The artist is cursed with many things true
But one thing it is not ever is bored
Disturbed – yes, distressed – of course
Isolated and tortured: yes
but never bored
For there are not enough hours
Nor ever enough days
Not enough support or enough ways to paint all you want
    to paint and draw all you can
To read and explore all you want to expand
To learn all you desire
To write all the stories that stock your head
There couldn't be enough hours in your life even if you
    never touched your bed
An artist is much and understands great depths
But one thing it cannot comprehend is
                    Bored.

Infinite Darkness

The depths of this mind are dark and true
That which no one else should be let in
The maze of darkness is infinite there
That to which one can ever fully leave
Lest they are plucking viscous webs of despair off them
Every step of the way
Still never returning to what they once were
Advise then to keep these doors sealed
Al fresco is no place for this webbing
Innocent hearts needn't be sanded
Leave that to the wood.

Can you Feel It?

Something magical is happening here. Can you feel it?
Something amazing right here right now
The birds are singing , do you even hear them?
The children are playing, just listen
The Earth is praising your life, your breath is your
present
Do you feel it ?
Beyond the hustle and bustle, beyond the running late,
the have to dos, the likes, the posts, the emails, beyond
getting gas
 Just pause and listen.
Your breath is buzzing ,the birds are singing, people are
breathing around you, as free as they come
Something magical is happening around you
Can you feel it?
Just take a moment, stop and listen.

Life Shouts

When life shouts at you make your voice smaller than a
whisper
Isolate, be quite, meditate and pray
Silence the noise and stop and listen
For there's something you must be missin.

End

So perhaps it's the end yet maybe it's the beginning
For one thing I know is this mind keeps me spinning

The petal is the goal
To be in tune enough with the pureness of soul

So look out for more, hopefully just the petal
                Will grace the page like classics
                        instead of heavy metal
          No promises though, control I have not
Just the pressing of keys like pen making plot.